The House Across the Street

The truth was never across the street... it was inside the house.

by
Jessy Mrani Gudoian

ISBNs:

eBook: 978-1-972458-24-2

Paperback: 978-1-972458-25-9

Hardback: 978-1-972458-26-6

Published by:
Book Publisher House

Table of Contents

Prologue

The Night Leslie Carter Died

The wind off the ocean was colder than it should have been for early spring.

Leslie Carter wrapped her arms around herself as she walked down the narrow coastal road, heels clicking against the pavement in sharp echoes that bounced off the dark water below the cliffs.

The town of Blackwater Cove slept early. By ten o'clock the streets were usually empty.

Tonight they were silent.

Too silent.

She checked her phone again.

No new messages from Nate.

Her stomach tightened. The fight earlier still replayed in her mind.

"Why do you keep talking to her?" she had snapped at him across the dinner table.

Nate had looked confused.

"Talking to who?"

"Sarah."

He had laughed it off.

"She's just the neighbor."

But Leslie had seen the way Sarah smiled at him. Too long. Too warm.

And then there was Steven.

Sarah's husband.

Leslie shivered.

Something about him made her skin crawl.

He watched people the way predators watched prey.

Earlier tonight she had noticed him standing in the shadows of his enormous house across the street.

Watching.

Always watching.

Leslie quickened her pace.

The road curved along the cliffs where the waves slammed violently against jagged rocks thirty feet below.

The wind howled.

Behind her—

Footsteps.

She froze.

The footsteps stopped too.

Her heart began pounding.

"Hello?" she called, her voice shaky.

No answer.

She turned slowly.

Nothing.

Just darkness.

Then a figure stepped out from the shadows.

Tall. Still. Watching her.

Her breath caught in her throat.

"You?" she whispered.

The figure moved closer.

Moonlight revealed a familiar face.

Leslie's eyes widened.

"You shouldn't be here," she said.

The person tilted their head slightly.

"You weren't supposed to know."

"What are you talking about?"

The wind roared louder now.

Leslie took a step backward.

Another.

Her heel slipped slightly on loose gravel.

"Stay away from me."

The figure kept coming.

Slow.

Calm.

Terrifyingly calm.

"You don't understand," the voice said quietly.

Leslie's heart pounded harder.

"Yes I do," she said. "I saw you watching him."

Silence.

Then the figure smiled.

A cold, empty smile.

"I can't let you ruin everything."

Leslie tried to run.

But the hands came fast.

Too fast.

Grabbing her arms.

She screamed.

The sound was swallowed by the crashing waves below.

For a moment they struggled.

Then—

A shove.

Her body tipped backward toward the edge of the cliff.

Her last sight before falling was the man standing above her.

Watching.

Expressionless.

Then Leslie Carter disappeared into the darkness below.

And the ocean swallowed her scream.

Chapter 1: The Man Who Owned the Town

The road narrowed as it curved toward the sea, the asphalt giving way to gravel that whispered beneath tires. Salt hung thick in the air. Houses stood spaced apart, their paint softened by sun and wind, their windows reflecting the restless grey-blue of the ocean beyond. Nothing moved quickly here. Even the gulls seemed to glide instead of flap.

The moving truck coughed to a halt in front of the empty house.

Nate Reynolds jumped down from the passenger side before the engine fully died, boots hitting the ground with a solid thud. He took in the place in one sweeping glance, the wide porch, the clean siding, the stretch of water visible just beyond the neighboring roofs and let out a low whistle.

"This is it," he said, more to himself than to Leslie.

Leslie Carter, his girlfriend who had come here to help him move and enjoy a vacation with him, stepped out more slowly, one hand still resting on the door. The breeze caught her hair, pushing it across her face. She brushed it back and looked at the house, then at the quiet street, then toward the distant line where the ocean met the sky.

"It's… quiet," she said.

Nate grinned, already moving toward the back of the truck. "That's the point." He rolled up the door with a metallic rattle, sunlight spilling over stacked boxes and wrapped furniture. "Compared to Chicago, it's a fresh start. New place. No noise, no chaos. Just us, even so briefly." He winked at her on purpose. She grinned at him.

Leslie nodded, but her gaze lingered on the neighboring houses. Curtains shifted. A figure disappeared from a window. The street settled again as if nothing had moved at all.

Nate didn't seem to notice. He grabbed the first box, balancing it easily against his hip. "Come on," he called over his shoulder. "Let's make this house a home."

By the time the sun dipped lower, casting long shadows across the street, the front door stood open and the house had begun to fill with the shape of a life. A couch angled toward the window. Boxes stacked in uneven towers. The faint smell of cardboard and fresh paint.

A knock sounded against the open doorframe.

Nate turned, wiping his hands on his jeans. "Hey—"

A man stood there, broad-shouldered, smiling as if he'd been waiting for this moment all day. Beside him, a woman with dark hair and an easy posture held a covered dish.

"Figured you might not feel like cooking tonight," she said, lifting it slightly.

"I'm Steven," the man added, extending a hand. "This is my wife, Sarah. We're right across the street."

Nate shook his hand firmly. "Nate." He gestured toward his girlfriend, "This is Leslie. And yeah, you're a lifesaver."

More neighbors drifted over in ones and twos, drawn by the open door and the arrival of someone new. Mrs. Eleanor Whitcombe from number twelve came clutching a tin of still-warm lemon biscuits, her silver hair pinned neatly beneath a pale blue scarf. Close behind her came Harold Bennett, the retired postman from two doors down, his weathered hands tucked into the pockets of his brown coat as he offered a quiet but genuine welcome. Soon after, Lila and Marcus Patel appeared with their young daughter Anya, who shyly hid behind her mother's leg while peeking curiously at the newcomer.

Names were exchanged in a cheerful blur, hands shaken, introductions repeated, small stories shared. Laughter filled the entryway, rising and falling like music, and before long the house seemed to breathe with life, its walls absorbing the warmth of voices, the easy familiarity of neighbors turning strangers into something closer to friends.

"Good people," Nate said closing the door after the last of them had gone. "This place? It's going to be great."

Leslie looked around the half-unpacked room, then toward the darkened window of the house from across the street, Steven's mansion. "Yeah," she said quietly.

Six weeks later, the rhythm of Blackwater Cove had settled around them. Leslie had extended her vacation on Nate's insistence.

Morning light spilled through the windows at the same angle each day. The sound of the ocean slipped into every room. Nate moved through the house barefoot, easy and at home, as if he'd always belonged there.

Across the street, the glass walls of Steven Callahan's mansion reflected the fading light.

Inside, the house stood silent.

Steven stood near the window, one hand resting lightly against the cool surface of the glass.

The lights in Nate's house flickered on.

A shadow passed by the window. Then another.

Steven leaned forward, his reflection dissolving into the dark as his focus sharpened.

There he was.

Nate Reynolds.

Crossing the living room, barefoot, a glass in hand. His shoulders loose, his steps unhurried. He moved like nothing in the world pressed against him.

Like nothing could.

Steven's jaw tightened.

Behind him, a soft voice broke the stillness.

"You're doing it again."

He turned.

Sarah stood at the top of the staircase, wrapped in a silk robe, one hand resting lightly on the banister. Her dark hair fell over her shoulders, catching what little light remained.

For a moment, neither of them spoke. Then Sarah went about her business as if this was nothing short of usual.

Steven glanced back toward the window but now Nate was nowhere in sight.

Chapter 2: The Wife Everyone Talked About

People in Blackwater Cove had a lot to say about Sarah Callahan.

Mostly when she wasn't around.

"She married him for the money."

"She could be his daughter."

"That marriage won't last."

In cafés, at the marina, in whispered conversations behind half-lowered hands, Sarah's name was often followed by speculation, suspicion, or a knowing smirk.

But the truth was far simpler.

Sarah loved Steven.

When she met him five years earlier at a charity gala, the room had been alive with laughter, clinking glasses, and polished conversation. Crystal chandeliers cast soft light across expensive suits and evening gowns, but Steven stood slightly apart from it all. He held a drink he hadn't touched, his posture composed, his expression distant like someone present in body but not entirely in spirit.

While others saw wealth, Sarah saw the quiet weight he carried.

Loneliness.

It wasn't dramatic or obvious. It lived in the small things, the way his gaze drifted beyond the crowd, the way he paused before responding to someone as if deciding whether the effort was worth it. Most people avoided that kind of emptiness. Sarah didn't.

She had always been drawn to broken things.

Now, years later, she stood in the sunlit kitchen of their home in Blackwater Cove, the scent of fresh coffee curling through the air. The wide windows opened the room to the ocean beyond, where the water shimmered and rolled in slow, endless motion. Morning light spilled across the marble counters, warming the cool surfaces with a soft gold glow.

At the long island, Steven sat with a stack of financial reports spread before him. Pages turned in his hands with quiet precision, the soft rustle the only sound he made. His focus was absolute, as though the world beyond those numbers could wait.

Sarah poured coffee into two mugs. Steam curled upward, briefly catching the light before fading into the air.

"You're quiet today," she said, her voice gentle as she crossed the room.

"I'm working," Steven replied without looking up.

"You're always working."

He turned another page, the corner of the paper brushing against the polished surface of the counter.

Sarah let out a soft breath, placing one of the mugs beside his hand. She didn't push further. Instead, her eyes drifted toward the window, where movement caught her attention.

"Have you had the chance to meet the new neighbor again?"

Steven's eyes flickered upward for the briefest moment before returning to the report.

"Not after the first day they came here."

"Nate seems nice."

That time, he looked at her fully, his gaze steady and assessing.

"Why do you think that?"

"I spoke to him yesterday," Sarah said, a small smile forming as she remembered. "While walking Luna." At the sound of her name, their golden retriever lifted her head from where she lay near the doorway. Luna's tail thumped against the floor in a slow, rhythmic beat, her ears perking with quiet interest. Sarah's expression softened as she glanced down at her. "He just moved here from Chicago."

Steven leaned back slightly, studying her now with more attention.

"And?"

"He seems normal."

The word lingered in the air between them, as if it didn't quite belong in this place.

Steven's gaze sharpened. "Normal people don't move to Blackwater Cove."

Sarah gave a quiet laugh, moving to stand beside him.

"You did."

His expression shifted, something guarded flickering beneath the surface. The reminder of his own choices, his own past, settled between them like an unspoken weight.

"I built this town," he said, his voice even, controlled.

Sarah picked up her coffee, her fingers wrapping around the warmth of the mug. She placed the other hand lightly on his arm, grounding, steadying.

"Yes," she said softly. "I know."

Chapter 3: The Neighbor Across the Street

Nate Reynolds moved to Blackwater Cove because he needed a reset.

His tech company had sold for more money than he could spend in three lifetimes.

And after ten brutal years in Chicago's corporate war zone, he wanted quiet.

The coastal town seemed perfect.

Small. Private. Beautiful.

The only thing he hadn't expected was the mansion across the street.

And the man who owned it.

Steven Callahan had introduced himself the day Nate moved in.

The handshake had been firm.

But his eyes had lingered a little too long.

Studying him.

Evaluating him.

Nate had learned to recognize powerful men.

Steven was one of the most dangerous types.

The kind who controlled everything.

Now Nate stood outside, watering plants, when he heard footsteps.

He turned.

Sarah Callahan approached with a golden retriever happily pulling the leash.

"Morning," she called.

"Morning," Nate replied with a smile.

The dog ran toward him.

"Well, hello there."

Sarah laughed.

"Luna likes you."

"Apparently."

They stood talking casually about the weather, the town, and restaurants nearby.

Nothing unusual.

Nothing inappropriate.

Just neighbors chatting.

But from the second-floor window of the mansion across the street—

Steven Callahan watched every second.

And as Sarah laughed at something Nate said—

A slow, dangerous thought began forming inside Steven's mind.

One that would soon destroy all of their lives.

Chapter 4: Smiles That Meant Nothing

Sarah was the type of woman who remembered names and asked about people's mothers and held doors open even when her hands were full. In Blackwater Cove, where wealth had hardened most faces into polite masks, Sarah's friendliness stood out like a candle in a dark room.

It was why women judged her.

It was why men lingered when she spoke.

And it was why Steven watched her the way he watched the stock market waiting for a dip, a betrayal, a sign.

That morning, Sarah found Nate by the mailbox at the end of his driveway, sorting through a stack of glossy brochures he clearly didn't want.

"Looks like the town already loves you," she said, nodding at the paper.

Nate smirked. "I think the town loves my address."

She laughed, and it was an easy sound, the kind of laugh that belonged to someone who still believed the world was mostly safe.

"You'll learn fast," Sarah said. "If you go to the marina café, don't sit near the window unless you're prepared to be watched."

Nate raised a brow. "By who?"

Sarah pointed without thinking.

Across the street, behind the sunlit glare of glass, Steven's silhouette stood motionless in the upstairs window.

Sarah's smile faltered for half a second.

Then she lifted her hand and waved at her husband like nothing was wrong.

Steven did not wave back.

Nate's expression changed not fear, not exactly. More like recognition. Like he understood what kind of man Steven was without anyone needing to say it out loud.

"You okay?" Nate asked quietly.

Sarah forced brightness back into her voice. "Of course. Steven is just… Steven."

But as she spoke, she felt it, the shift. The thin thread of tension that always ran under her marriage like a wire ready to snap.

They talked a little longer, mostly about harmless things: where the closest grocery store was, why the town's sidewalks were uneven, how the ocean air made everything smell like salt and money.

Then Sarah's phone vibrated.

A message from Steven.

Where are you?

Sarah stared at it. She hadn't been gone more than ten minutes.

She typed quickly.

Walking Luna Baby. Talking to Nate for a minute. Be home soon.

She slipped the phone back into her pocket and tried not to let Nate see the way her shoulders tightened.

Nate didn't say anything. He just offered her a soft, sympathetic smile, like he already knew what it meant to live under someone else's gaze.

As Sarah turned to leave, she looked up at the mansion again.

The upstairs window was empty.

But she could still feel Steven watching.

And inside the glass house, Steven watched Sarah walk away, her hair catching the sunlight, her laughter fading as she crossed the street back toward him.

He didn't see a neighborly conversation.

He saw a performance.

And every smile she gave Nate, every little tilt of her head, felt like a knife he couldn't pull out.

Chapter 5: The House That Raised Him

30 years ago...

The polished banister caught the light the way a blade might, hard, deliberate, without softness. A young Steven Callahan stood at its base with a damp cloth in his hands, watching the wood as though it might judge him. His knuckles stung from the scrubbing, the skin split and raw, but he didn't stop until his father's footsteps echoed across the upstairs landing.

"Again."

The word carried down like a verdict.

Steven lowered his gaze and pressed the cloth back to the wood.

Present day...

Steven Callahan had been taught to keep his hands clean.

Not literally, his father had made him scrub floors until his knuckles bled when he was a boy, as punishment for leaving a single fingerprint on the polished banister.

Clean in the other sense.

Clean reputation. Clean name. Clean life.

The Callahan men were not the type to stumble in public. They did not cry. They did not beg. They did not admit weakness. They certainly did not admit desire.

At the dinner table, silence had been its own kind of discipline. His mother moved like a shadow between courses, placing plates down without sound, her eyes lowered, her voice reserved for when his father demanded it. Steven learned early that sound attracted attention, and attention invited scrutiny.

So he learned to move without drawing breath.

Steven's childhood home had been all sharp angles and hushed voices. His mother spoke only when spoken to. His father's approval was something Steven learned to chase like air, necessary, invisible, impossible to hold.

That approval came in small, fleeting gestures: a nod after a well-delivered answer, a brief "acceptable" after an exam, silence, the rare kind that meant he hadn't failed.

He carried that hunger into every room he entered.

He sat in church every Sunday since he was fourteen, with his hands clenched so tightly his nails cut crescents into his palms, listening to the sermon about temptation, about sin, about the ruin of men who let themselves become "something unnatural".

The preacher's voice rose and fell, sharp and accusing, but Steven heard only the heartbeat in his ears. He kept his head bowed, though not in prayer. Not exactly.

He had looked at his father's profile, the rigid jaw, the cold calm and understood with sick clarity that if his father ever learned his secret that he had been burying for some time, he would be destroyed.

Not punished.

Destroyed.

So Steven did what he'd been trained to do.

He stayed quiet.

He excelled. He became untouchable. He built himself into a man no one questioned. A man no one dared to see through.

He learned to smile at the right moments, to extend the right hand, to make the right promises. He learned how to build a life that looked effortless from the outside, even as it was constructed brick by careful brick, each one placed to conceal the ones beneath.

Marriage was part of that.

It had been presented to him like a contract, like a merger between two families that shared values, ambition, and a mutual understanding of appearances. The woman who became his first wife had been elegant, poised, and perfectly suited to stand beside him in photographs.

There had been no passion in the beginning. Only alignment.

The first marriage had been practical, strategic, a union of reputations. It lasted long enough to produce James and Kris and a legacy that looked perfect from the outside.

Photographs showed a family that smiled easily, children pressed between parents who stood close enough to suggest intimacy. Guests at dinners praised the Callahans for their stability. Their home became a model of success, admired for its order.

Behind closed doors, Steven measured everything.

Time. Words. Silence.

Then it cracked.

It didn't shatter all at once. It started in small fractures. his wife lingering too long at the window, her questions becoming sharper, her patience thinning. She asked about him in ways he didn't know how to answer. She wanted warmth where he offered structure.

And structure, he realized, was not enough.

His first wife had wanted warmth. Steven had offered order.

He would come home late, the house dim, the children asleep, and she would sit across from him, her hands folded, her expression searching. She would ask him to stay longer, to talk more, to be something he had never learned how to become.

And when she left, Steven had felt relief, not heartbreak. Relief that the performance of loving her and wanting to be home around her had ended.

He didn't chase her.

He didn't plead.

He adjusted.

Life resumed with fewer expectations. Fewer demands. Fewer moments where he had to pretend.

The house quieted again, but this time the silence felt like control instead of absence.

Sarah entered his life the way a well-timed asset enters a portfolio, useful, predictable, and advantageous.

Sarah was different.

Sarah was younger. Easier to shape. Easier to present. A beautiful symbol that screamed normal to every gossiping mouth in town.

She smiled often, laughed easily, and spoke to people as though they mattered. When she looked at Steven, there was no hesitation, no suspicion, only admiration.

And that admiration was intoxicating in its simplicity.

With Sarah, he didn't have to explain himself. She filled in the blanks with her own assumptions, seeing in him what he needed her to see.

And when she looked at him with devotion, Steven almost believed he could become the man he pretended to be.

Almost.

But now—

Now there was Nate Reynolds across the street, existing too loudly. Too freely. Too close.

Steven stood in his home office, staring at his computer screen.

The room was immaculate. Dark wood desk. Carefully arranged books. A view that overlooked the street below like a vantage point rather than a comfort.

The screen glowed softly, casting light across his face.

He hadn't meant to search. The thought had simply slipped out of a locked place in his mind and into his fingers.

A name. A photo. A quick search.

Nate Reynolds' public profile appeared: a handful of articles about the company sale, a charity gala mention, a photo of Nate laughing at some event in Chicago, nice suit jacket open, tie loosened.

The image lingered longer than it should have.

Then he heard Sarah downstairs, humming as she moved around the kitchen.

The sound carried lightly, warm and unguarded. It didn't belong to the careful world Steven had built.

He closed the laptop quickly, as if it had caught him doing something filthy.

His heart was steady. His face calm.

Control, Steven reminded himself.

Control was not something he practiced occasionally, it was something he lived inside of, like a second skin.

It wasn't Nate that was the problem.

It was Sarah.

Sarah with her friendliness. Sarah with her careless smiles. Sarah with her conversations that looked harmless to anyone naïve enough to believe in harmlessness.

Steven walked to the window again.

Across the street, Nate stepped onto his front porch, squinting into the sun.

The man moved without hesitation, without awareness of the space he occupied in someone else's carefully constructed world. He stretched slightly, as if the day belonged to him.

Steven's jaw tightened.

Not because Nate was a threat in the traditional sense.

But because he was something Steven had never allowed himself to be.

Uncontained.

Steven told himself he was studying a threat.

He told himself his anger was righteous.

And as he stood there, something inside him shifted, quietly, permanently, like a lock turning.

He didn't yet know what he would do.

But he knew the direction his mind was moving.

And it frightened him, because it felt like relief.

Chapter 6: Leslie Carter

After the warm welcome at Nate's house, Sarah met Leslie on a Friday afternoon when she stepped out of her car and nearly collided with her. Sarah was in oversized sunglasses and a white linen jumpsuit.

"Oh—sorry!" Sarah said automatically.

Leslie paused, tilting her sunglasses down just enough to inspect her.

For a moment, Sarah braced for the coldness so common in town.

Instead, Leslie smiled wide. "Don't be. I wasn't watching where I was going."

Her voice had the smooth confidence of someone used to being listened to.

"You're Sarah, right?" Leslie asked.

Sarah blinked. "Guilty as charged."

"Nate talks about you," Leslie said, and then laughed at Sarah's expression. "In a normal way. Like 'the neighbor who saved me from buying moldy avocados' way."

Sarah laughed despite herself. "I'm glad my greatest contribution is fruit advice."

Leslie's smile grew. "You're cute. I like you."

Sarah felt warmth spread through her chest. "You're Leslie."

"Guilty." Leslie pushed her suitcase the rest of the way up the steps. "I'm only here for a couple weeks. Work stuff, Nate stuff, sunshine stuff."

Sarah glanced toward the mansion across the street out of habit.

The upstairs office window reflected blue sky.

No silhouette.

Still, she lowered her voice slightly. "Welcome to Blackwater Cove. Just… ignore most of what people say."

Leslie leaned closer, conspiratorial. "Oh honey, I'm from Chicago. I can handle small-town snakes."

Sarah smiled.

And across the street, behind glass and money, Steven Callahan watched the entire interaction through binoculars he pretended he didn't own.

Leslie's presence should have reassured him.

See? A rational voice might have said. Nate has a girlfriend. Sarah is just being friendly. There's nothing to worry about.

But Steven didn't feel reassured.

He felt… irritated.

Because Leslie's presence didn't erase the image in his mind of Sarah and Nate standing too close, laughing too easily.

Because jealousy wasn't logical.

It was hunger.

And Steven had been starving for years, pretending it is okay for somebody else beside him to have the attention, the fame and more money.

That night, Sarah mentioned Leslie casually while setting the table.

"Nate's girlfriend is here," she said, placing plates down carefully like she could arrange peace with porcelain. "She seems sweet."

Steven's fork paused midair.

"She's staying with him?"

Sarah looked up, puzzled. "Yes. They're dating."

Steven forced a neutral hum, his face perfectly composed.

But inside, a thought flickered sharp and unwanted.

He swallowed hard.

Sarah reached across the table and squeezed Steven's hand. "We should invite them over," she said brightly. "A welcome dinner."

Steven stared at Sarah's hand on his, her fingers warm, trusting.

And he realized something that made his stomach clench.

If he said no, Sarah would question why.

And Steven could not afford questions.

"Why not," he said smoothly. "Invite them."

Sarah beamed, relieved.

Steven smiled back.

And under the table, his hand tightened into a fist.

Chapter 7: Welcome Dinner

The dinner was Sarah's idea, though that was only part of the story. Steven remembered the way she'd stood in the kitchen that afternoon, flipping through recipes with a quiet determination, as if the evening itself depended on her getting it right.

He watched from the doorway, drink in hand, as she worked. She didn't notice him at first. She rarely did when she was like this, focused, present, trying to make something beautiful out of a moment most people would let pass without effort.

Sarah moved with practiced ease, pulling herbs from a bowl, tasting a sauce with the tip of a spoon, adjusting seasoning without measuring. The air filled with the smell of garlic and rosemary, warm bread, and something sweet baking in the oven.

Her hair had slipped loose from its pins, a strand falling against her cheek. She brushed it away with the back of her wrist, leaving a faint smear of flour.

Steven didn't move to help.

He stood there, watching.

He'd learned long ago that helping could be mistaken for something else.

Partnership.

And partnership had never come naturally to him.

* * *

Long before polished floors and quiet wealth, there had been a boy in a small, dim house who learned early what it meant to be alone in a room full of expectations.

His father spoke in commands, not conversations. His mother measured silence like it was something fragile, something to be preserved.

Steven remembered standing on a chair too short for the counter, his small hands wrapped around a bottle of soap while his father pointed out every streak left behind on the glass.

"Again," his father would say.

And again.

Until the reflection looked the way it was supposed to.

Perfect.

Immaculate.

Unquestionable.

That was the language Steven learned.

* * *

The doorbell rang, sharp and punctual.

Steven's gaze shifted back to the present as Sarah wiped her hands and hurried toward the entryway, her expression lighting up before she even opened the door.

Nate stood on the threshold, a bottle of wine in one hand, his posture relaxed but alert in a way Steven immediately recognized.

Beside him, Leslie carried a small gift bag, her smile easy, practiced.

"Housewarming gift," she said, offering it to Sarah. "Or is it dinner-hosting gift? I don't know the rules."

Sarah laughed, genuine and warm. "There are no rules. Come in."

Steven watched the exchange without moving.

Nate's eyes moved across the space, taking in the structure, the materials, the placement of objects. Not intrusive. Not obvious.

Just observant.

Leslie lingered a moment longer, her gaze catching on details, artwork, finishes, the quiet language of wealth that spoke louder than any conversation.

Then Steven stepped forward.

"Welcome," he said.

His voice was even. Controlled. Polished.

A tone he had spent years refining into something that revealed nothing.

Nate extended his hand. "Steven. Thanks for having us."

Their handshake was firm.

Measured.

Steven felt it, strength, confidence, the absence of hesitation.

It reminded him of other men he'd once known.

Men who didn't flinch.

Men who took what they wanted.

Men who had either succeeded… or disappeared trying.

* * *

Steven had once shaken hands like that before.

The first time he met his first wife, it had been at a business function though it had been called a charity gala to soften the truth of it.

She had stood near a window, her reflection overlapping the city lights behind her. Not smiling. Not posing.

Just watching.

She hadn't approached him. He had approached her.

"You look like you don't belong here," he'd said.

She'd looked at him like she'd heard that before.

"And you do?"

That had been the beginning.

Not of romance.

Of recognition.

They had married quickly. Efficiently. Like two people agreeing to a contract they both understood but neither truly questioned.

For a while, it had worked.

Dinner tables like this one. Conversations that sounded real enough to pass. A house that looked like something worth staying in.

But Steven remembered the distance growing in small increments.

The way she stopped asking questions.

The way she stopped looking at him the way she once had.

And the day she left, she didn't shout.

She didn't cry.

She simply placed her keys on the table and said, "I can't live like this anymore."

Steven hadn't stopped her.

Partnership had never been something he knew how to hold onto.

* * *

"Leslie," Leslie said now, offering her hand. "Thanks for inviting us."

Steven nodded as he took it. "My pleasure."

They moved to the dining room.

The table had been set with precision, plates aligned, glasses placed with intention, candles burning low and steady.

Sarah watched them all with quiet satisfaction, like a conductor pleased with the first notes of an orchestra.

She laughed at Nate's comments, her laughter light and natural.

Steven noticed how easily it came.

How freely it was given.

Sarah poured water for Nate before she poured for herself.

Across the table, Leslie noticed too.

She said nothing.

But her eyes tracked the movement, the small choices that spoke louder than words.

Sarah caught her looking once and offered a soft, apologetic smile, as if to say it didn't mean anything.

Leslie returned the smile.

But hers carried weight.

Not hostility.

Not yet.

Just awareness.

* * *

The meal unfolded in careful progression.

Steven spoke when necessary.

Silence was his preference. Silence gave him control. Silence allowed him to observe.

He studied Nate while pretending to focus on his plate. Watched how he spoke, how he paused, how he answered without rushing.

Nate spoke about Chicago. About the pressure. The hours. The decision to sell his company.

Steven asked questions that seemed casual.

"How much did you sell for?"

"What's next?"

"How long do you plan to stay?"

Each question was measured. Each answer filed away.

Nate responded without hesitation, but his awareness never dropped.

He knew what this was.

Men like Nate always did.

Leslie stepped in at times, softening edges, redirecting conversation, smoothing over pauses that might otherwise grow uncomfortable.

Sarah watched Steven.

She didn't interrupt.

But she felt the shift in him, the subtle tightening that others might miss.

She always noticed when something was off.

It was one of the reasons Steven had married her.

* * *

The memory came back uninvited.

The house before this one.

The silence that lingered in rooms that used to echo with conversation.

His first marriage hadn't ended in betrayal.

It had ended in absence.

She had once told him, "You don't let anyone in."

And he had replied, "That's not true."

But it had been.

Even then.

Even before he knew how to name it.

* * *

When dessert came, Sarah excused herself to the kitchen.

Leslie followed shortly after.

Nate remained.

And for the first time all evening, the room quieted.

Steven swirled the drink in his glass, the liquid catching the light as it moved.

Nate leaned back slightly in his chair.

"Beautiful house," he said.

Steven nodded. "It serves its purpose."

Nate's mouth curved faintly. "That's an interesting way to describe a home."

Steven felt the words settle somewhere deeper than intended.

"A home," he said, "is what you make it."

Nate studied him. "And what did you make yours?"

Steven's gaze sharpened.

"Successful."

Nate's smile faltered just a fraction. "Right."

A beat passed.

Then Nate said, more carefully, "Sarah seems… happy."

Steven's grip tightened around the glass.

"She is," he said, too quickly.

Nate held his gaze a moment longer than necessary.

Then looked away.

In the kitchen, Sarah laughed.

The sound drifted into the dining room, light, warm, effortless.

Steven heard it.

He imagined it.

* * *

He misinterpreted it.

And in that moment, he decided something without fully deciding it.

This dinner wasn't a welcome.

It was a warning.

* * *

Chapter 8: The Watcher

Steven didn't sleep.

He lay beside Sarah in the dark, listening to the soft rhythm of her breathing, measuring it the way he measured everything, steady, predictable, under control.

But his mind kept replaying the dinner.

Sarah's laugh.

Nate's smile.

Leslie's eyes, sharp, assessing, too aware.

Steven stared at the ceiling until the first hint of dawn turned the room from black to gray. Then he rose quietly, dressed without turning on a light, and walked down the hall to his office.

He opened the bottom drawer of his desk.

Inside: a black case, foam-lined, precise.

Binoculars.

He told himself they were for the ocean, for watching boats, for watching storms roll in, a rich man's toy.

He lifted them like a ritual.

Crossed the room.

Pulled aside the curtain.

And aimed them at the house across the street.

Nate's lights were off.

A shadow moved behind the upstairs window.

Steven's breath slowed, controlled, almost reverent.

The binoculars sharpened the world into crisp detail, the line of Nate's shoulder, the casual way he moved, the freedom in his body as if he'd never been told to make himself smaller.

Steven felt something surge, anger, yes.

A door opened.

Leslie emerged into the upstairs hallway wearing one of Nate's shirts.

Leslie crossed to the window, unaware she was being watched.

She stretched, yawned, turned away.

Steven lowered the binoculars.

His jaw flexed.

The thought should have soothed him.

Instead it made his skin crawl with a fury he didn't understand.

He stood there longer than he meant to, still staring at the dark house as if it might explain itself. The silence of the street felt intentional, like everything had paused just for him to notice. Somewhere in the distance, a gull cried over the ocean, and even that sound felt intrusive.

Steven went to his desk, opened his laptop, and pulled up the security camera feed for the front of his property.

His cameras were state-of-the-art. Every angle covered. Every movement recorded.

He zoomed in on the street.

He couldn't see Nate's front door, too far, too much landscaping.

So Steven did what he always did when the world didn't give him what he wanted.

He changed the world.

Within an hour, his head of security had a call.

By noon, two new cameras were installed, officially "for wildlife monitoring" along the property line.

Unofficially, to watch the house across the street.

That afternoon, Sarah came home with bags from the boutique in town, cheeks pink from the ocean wind.

She smiled when she saw Steven at the kitchen island, and for a second she looked the way she used to look, like she believed she was safe here.

"You're home early," she said.

Steven didn't look up from his phone.

"Work is handled," he said.

Sarah hesitated. "I was thinking, maybe I'll go for a walk later. Luna's been restless."

Steven's thumbs stilled.

"A walk where?"

Sarah blinked. "Around the neighborhood."

Steven finally lifted his eyes.

"Alone?"

Sarah's patience flashed, bright and quick. "With the dog."

Steven's smile didn't reach his eyes. "Of course."

Sarah turned toward the stairs, her bags rustling.

And Steven watched her leave, already calculating how long it would take her to cross the street.

He didn't call it obsession.

Steven called it protection.

But the truth was simpler.

Steven couldn't stop watching.

And the more he watched, the more the story in his head grew teeth.

It began to feel less like observation and more like construction, as if every glance was another brick in something inevitable. Something that was already happening whether anyone agreed to it or not.

Chapter 9: The Thing About Leslie

Leslie Carter was not the kind of woman who missed details.

She was polished, yes. Stylish, yes. But beneath the smooth surface was a mind that had spent years learning how to read rooms, how to detect danger disguised as charm.

It was why she'd succeeded in corporate spaces where men smiled and lied under the same breath.

It was why she didn't like Steven Callahan.

She'd felt it at the dinner, the temperature drop when Steven entered the room, the way his eyes skimmed over her like she was a piece of furniture.

Not dismissed exactly.

Assessed, measured.

And then the way he looked at Nate.

Leslie tried not to think about that part.

Because it didn't make sense.

After dinner, she told Nate in bed, "Your neighbor is… intense."

Nate laughed softly into the pillow. "He's the richest guy in town. Intense is probably part of the package."

Leslie propped herself on her elbow. "It's not just wealth. It's control."

Nate sighed. "He seems protective of Sarah."

Leslie's eyes narrowed. "Protective isn't the word I'd use."

Nate kissed her shoulder. "You're reading into it."

Leslie, frustrated, tried to understand how Nate did not see what was going on. Then added, "I think that he saw how Sarah was flirtatious with you and he didn't like it."

Nate looked at her in disbelief. "Stop making things up. Sarah was not flirtatious, she is just being friendly. I'm not the only one she is friendly to."

Leslie frowned. "How do you know that? Have you been watching her?"

Nate didn't say a word and decided to walk away because he couldn't deal with the accusations Leslie had made about their neighbors after just having a good time at their house one dinner.

Leslie lay there afterward, staring at the ceiling, replaying every moment again and again. Nate's dismissal of her concern did not calm her. It sharpened it. It made her feel like she was the only one paying attention in a room full of people choosing comfort over truth.

The next morning Leslie woke early and went out to the porch with coffee.

The ocean air was cool, the street quiet.

Across the street, the Callahan mansion gleamed like a blade.

Leslie stared at it.

Then she felt it, that prickling sensation at the back of her neck.

She turned slightly.

A curtain shifted upstairs.

And for a fraction of a second she saw Steven.

Watching her.

Leslie's grip tightened around the coffee mug.

She lifted her hand casually, as if waving at a neighbor.

The curtain didn't move again.

Steven didn't wave back.

Leslie forced herself to look away.

But the message had already landed.

He is watching this house.

And if he was watching the house, he was watching Nate.

A chill moved through Leslie that had nothing to do with the ocean breeze.

That afternoon, Leslie took a walk alone, letting Nate work in his office.

She passed Sarah near the mailbox.

Sarah smiled warmly. "Hey! How's your first week here going?"

Leslie studied her.

Sarah's friendliness seemed genuine. Almost too genuine for this town.

"You really like being kind, don't you?" Leslie asked lightly.

Sarah laughed. "It's easier than being cruel."

Leslie smiled back, but it didn't fully reach her eyes.

"Careful," she said.

Sarah's smile faltered. "About what?"

Leslie added, "Sarah, I honestly don't like the way you smile at Nate all the time and stop by his house."

Sarah stiffened. "I am sorry you are feeling this way, but Nate is just a neighbor. I am friendly to everyone and he is no exception."

The air between them tightened, polite on the surface but edged underneath, like something neither of them wanted to name.

Chapter 10: The Body

The town found Leslie Carter on a Monday.

That was how the story would be told for years afterward, as if Blackwater Cove itself had reached into the sea and pulled out a warning.

But the truth was, it wasn't the town.

It was a jogger.

A man named Harold Sykes, retired Coast Guard, who ran the cliff road every morning at six.

He saw something caught between rocks below the overlook, something pale and wrong.

At first he thought it was driftwood.

Then he saw hair and a body lying there not moving.

Harold called 911 with shaking hands.

By seven, police tape fluttered in the sea wind like yellow ribbon on a grave.

By eight, everyone knew.

And by nine, everyone was standing in little clusters at the marina café, whispering with the kind of excitement people tried to hide under horror.

Murder was rare in Blackwater Cove.

But scandal was a currency.

Sarah learned when she walked into the boutique and the women fell silent so quickly it was like the air had been snapped.

Her stomach tightened.

She pulled out her phone.

Three missed calls from Steven.

She called him back immediately.

He answered on the first ring.

"Where are you?" His voice was sharp.

"I'm at the boutique. Why?"

"Come home."

Sarah's throat tightened. "What's wrong?"

A pause.

Then Steven said, quietly, "There's been an incident."

Sarah hurried out, heart pounding.

She drove home with the radio off, hands tight on the wheel.

When she arrived, Steven stood outside on the front steps, dressed like a man going to court, dark suit, crisp shirt, perfect tie.

His face was calm.

Too calm.

Sarah rushed to him. "Steven, what happened?"

Steven looked at her with something like pity.

"Leslie Carter is dead."

The words hit Sarah like cold water.

"What?" she breathed. "No, how?"

Steven's hand landed on her shoulder, heavy, claiming.

"They found her near the cliffs."

Sarah's mind scrambled. "Oh my God. Nate—"

"Is being questioned," Steven cut in.

Sarah's breath hitched. "Questioned? Why?"

Steven's eyes flicked over her face slowly, as if memorizing her reaction.

"Because she was his girlfriend," he said. "And because it's what police do."

Sarah swallowed. "We should go—"

Steven's hand tightened on her shoulder. "No."

Sarah blinked. "Why not?"

Steven leaned closer, voice lowering.

"People will be watching," he murmured. "Let them watch something else."

Sarah stared at him.

"What do you mean?"

Steven's gaze moved past her, out toward the street.

Toward Nate's house.

Police cars.

Flashing lights.

A crowd.

Steven spoke softly, almost tender.

"In times like this," he said, "it's best not to give anyone a reason to misunderstand you."

Sarah's mouth went dry.

Something in Steven's tone felt wrong, like he wasn't warning her.

And across the street, Nate stood on his front lawn, face pale, eyes wild, surrounded by police.

He looked across the road.

His gaze locked with Sarah's.

For a moment, his expression begged her to understand: I didn't do this.

Sarah took a step forward instinctively.

Steven's hand stopped her.

Chapter 11: The Investigation

Detective Laura Medina arrived before noon.

She was younger than most people expected, mid-thirties, sharp-eyed, with her hair pulled into a neat bun that made her look severe even when she wasn't trying. She carried herself with quiet authority, the kind that came from years of dealing with cases where people lied easily and often. She had been transferred from the city a year earlier after a high-profile investigation had gone wrong, and Blackwater Cove had been presented to her as a quiet assignment. It was not quiet. It was simply quieter about its violence.

Medina walked through the crime scene at the cliffs, her eyes scanning every detail with methodical precision. The rocks were wet, still slick from the tide that had receded too recently. The tide line was high, suggesting the body had been in the water before it was found. Leslie's body had been battered by the waves, but there were still signs that told a different story.

A scrape on her forearm suggested she had tried to grab onto something. Dirt was lodged under her nails, and one nail was broken, torn unevenly. There was also a bruise forming around her wrist, faint but visible beneath the saltwater damage. Medina crouched slightly, studying the ground near the cliff edge.

Her gaze lifted upward. The fall had been too controlled, too precise. It felt less like an accident and more like something planned.

She turned to her partner.

"She is from out of town from what I have heard," Medina said. "What is she doing here in Blackwater Cove?"

"She is visiting her boyfriend," he replied.

Medina's mouth tightened slightly. "And do you have any information about him?"

"Yes. His name is Nate Reynolds, and he just moved here recently."

Medina exhaled slowly.

Medina stepped carefully around the edge of the cliff again, noticing something her partner had missed. A faint indentation in the soil near a patch of loose gravel suggested a second set of footprints had been partially washed away. She crouched and took photos, marking the location with a small flag from her kit.

"Someone else was here," she muttered.

Her partner frowned. "Tide could have erased it."

"Not like this," she replied. "This was recent interference. Someone disturbed the ground after the fall."

She straightened, looking out toward the sea. The wind was strong enough to carry sound inland, and she imagined how easily a struggle could have been hidden here.

"Call in forensics again," she added. "I want soil samples from deeper under the rocks."

As they walked back to the vehicle, Medina's phone buzzed. A preliminary background note on Nate Reynolds had come through. No criminal record. Clean employment history. Recent relocation. Nothing useful.

That worried her more than anything else.

Because in her experience, clean histories were either luck… or construction.

And construction meant intent.

Chapter 12: The First Lie

By afternoon, Medina was at Nate Reynolds' house.

Nate sat across from her with his hands clasped so tightly that his knuckles were white. His posture was rigid, as if he was holding himself together through sheer force of will rather than calm.

"I didn't kill her. It wasn't me," Nate said for the third time.

Medina watched him carefully, her expression steady and unreadable.

Grief looked different on different people, but Nate's grief had a frantic honesty to it, like his mind was still trying to catch up to a reality it refused to accept. His eyes kept shifting toward the window, then back to her, as though he expected someone else to walk in and correct the situation.

"When was the last time you saw her?" Medina asked.

"Last night," Nate said hoarsely. "We argued. It was stupid. She left."

"What was the argument about?"

Nate hesitated, his throat tightening as he swallowed.

Finally, Nate said, "She thought she thought something was weird about our neighbors."

Medina's pen paused over her notebook.

"Which neighbors?" she asked.

"The Callahans," Nate said. "Steven, Sarah."

Medina's eyes sharpened slightly. Her posture shifted just enough to signal attention without interruption.

"Why?" she asked.

Nate swallowed again, visibly uncomfortable now, as if saying it out loud gave it more weight than he wanted it to carry.

"Leslie thought Sarah was being too friendly with me, and she thought her husband has been monitoring my house."

Medina made a careful note, then looked back up.

"Did she have problems with Sarah?" she asked.

Nate shook his head quickly. "Besides mentioning her concern about how friendly she was, no. Sarah is kind. She's, she's harmless."

Medina leaned back slightly in her chair, studying him.

"Harmless people get accused all the time," she said evenly.

Nate stared at her. "Is she being accused?"

Medina responded, "We are looking at all possibilities."

Her tone stayed neutral, but her eyes remained fixed on him as if weighing every micro-reaction. In the background, a wall clock ticked too loudly for the silence in the room. A faint breeze pushed against the curtains, making them shift slightly, adding to the uneasy stillness.

Then she turned briefly toward her partner, who stood near the doorway, observing quietly with a folded notepad in hand.

"Any information you got about the neighbors?" she asked.

"The husband is Steven Callahan," he said. "Local royalty."

Medina's mouth tightened slightly at the phrase, but she did not comment on it.

"And the wife?" she asked.

"Sarah. Younger. Pretty. The town already doesn't like her."

Medina closed her notebook slowly, as if that detail mattered more than it should, not because it proved anything, but because it often shaped how people interpreted suspicion. She made a mental note to separate reputation from fact, something small towns rarely managed to do cleanly.

Nate shifted in his seat again, rubbing his palms together now as the initial shock gave way to restless anxiety. He looked like he wanted to say more but could not decide if it would help or make things worse. Medina noticed the hesitation and filed it away, along with the tension in his voice whenever Sarah's name came up.

Chapter 13: The Evidence

The call came early the next morning.

Sarah was in the kitchen pouring coffee when Steven's phone buzzed on the counter.

He glanced at the screen.

A faint smile touched his lips before disappearing.

Then he answered.

"Yes."

He listened quietly.

Sarah watched his expression shift into carefully constructed concern.

"I understand," Steven said.

He hung up slowly.

"What is it?" Sarah asked.

Steven sighed heavily. "The police found something at the cliffs."

Sarah's stomach tightened.

"What?"

Steven looked at her for a long moment.

"Your wallet and a necklace."

The room seemed to tilt.

"My wallet?" she whispered.

Steven nodded. "They found it near where Leslie's body was discovered."

Sarah's breath left her chest in a sharp burst. "Did they say it was my necklace?"

Steven didn't respond.

He simply studied her, like he always does, as if measuring reactions rather than sharing concern.

"I misplaced it two days ago after I got home but couldn't remember where I put it," she said quickly.

Steven leaned back against the counter.

"Your wallet was there, Sarah."

The way he said it made her feel suddenly exposed.

"And if you had it two days ago, how do you explain how it got there?"

Her heart began racing.

"It can't be," she said quickly. "My wallet is in my purse. I didn't go near the cliffs."

Steven studied her in silence.

There was no anger in his expression, only calculation, as though he was trying to fit her words into a pattern that refused to align.

Sarah noticed, for the first time, that he didn't offer reassurance.

Only observation.

The doorbell rang.

Both of them froze.

Steven walked slowly to the door and opened it.

Detective Laura Medina stood on the porch.

"Mr. Callahan," she said politely.

Steven stepped aside.

"Detective."

Her eyes shifted to Sarah.

"Mrs. Callahan."

Sarah's fingers tightened around her coffee mug.

Medina's voice was calm but direct.

"We need to ask you some questions."

As Medina stepped inside, her gaze briefly moved across the kitchen, taking in details without making it obvious. The calm order of the home stood out to her. Everything was placed with intention, nothing out of place, nothing rushed. It was the kind of environment that suggested control rather than chaos.

Steven gestured for them to sit, but Medina remained standing for a moment longer than necessary. She noticed Sarah's hesitation, the way her shoulders tightened slightly before she moved.

Medina opened her notebook but didn't immediately write. Instead, she watched both of them.

There was something in the dynamic that felt off, not in what they said, but in what wasn't being said between them. Steven spoke like someone used to directing conversations. Sarah spoke like someone waiting for permission to respond.

Medina finally sat down.

"I'll need details about your movements over the past forty-eight hours," she said evenly.

Outside, a car passed slowly on the street, and for a brief moment the sound filled the silence in the room.

No one spoke until it faded.

Chapter 14: The Interview

The police station in Blackwater Cove was small, too small for something like murder.

Sarah sat across from Detective Medina in a gray interview room that smelled faintly of old paper and stale coffee. Her hands rested on the metal table. They wouldn't stop shaking.

Medina slid a plastic evidence bag forward.

Inside was her wallet and a gold necklace.

Sarah stared at it.

"Those are both mine," she said quietly.

"When did you last see them?" Medina asked.

"I thought my wallet was in my purse, and two days ago I realized my necklace was missing," Sarah said. "I couldn't remember where I put it."

Medina wrote something down.

"Did you go near the cliffs this week?"

"No."

"Did you have any conflict with Leslie Carter?"

"No… I mean yes, kind of, but not really."

Medina watched her carefully.

"Can you elaborate?"

"She didn't like that I was friendly with her boyfriend. She told me to stay away."

"Did you have any romantic involvement with Nate Reynolds?"

Sarah's head snapped up.

"No."

Medina observed her closely.

"You spent time with him."

"We're neighbors," Sarah said.

"Your husband said you spoke frequently."

Sarah's stomach twisted.

"Yes, but only as neighbors."

Medina leaned back slightly.

"The necklace and wallet place you at the scene."

Sarah's chest tightened.

"I didn't kill her."

Medina didn't respond. She simply noted the response.

A faint sound from the hallway echoed into the room, footsteps passing by, then fading again. Sarah glanced briefly toward the door as if hoping someone would interrupt, then looked back down at her hands.

Medina noticed the hesitation.

It wasn't dramatic. It wasn't loud. But it was consistent.

She closed her notebook halfway, then reopened it again, shifting her approach slightly.

"Did anyone else have access to your belongings?" she asked.

"My housekeeper sometimes," Sarah said softly. "But she doesn't touch personal items."

Outside the room, another officer paused briefly, glancing through the window before moving on.

Sarah noticed that too.

The feeling of being observed settled deeper into her posture, making her shoulders draw in slightly as if she were trying to take up less space. Sarah looked distraught as if she would throw up any second. Medina noticed it but didn't say anything.

Medina nodded but didn't comment.

Because detectives didn't deal in comfort.

They dealt in patterns.

And right now a pattern was forming around Sarah that Medina knew all too well.

Steven was waiting outside the interrogation room.

Sarah came out crying, looking tired and they both drove home.

On their drive back home, the silence was heavier that death.

Steven hadn't asked a single question and Sarah didn't justify nor explained herself.

Once home, Steven sat in his office watching the news coverage of Leslie's death.

The reporter stood near the cliffs, wind whipping her hair as she spoke.

"Authorities have confirmed new evidence linking a local resident to the crime scene…"

Steven muted the television.

His reflection stared back at him from the dark screen.

Calm. Controlled. Perfect.

He had always been good at controlling everything around him.

It was how he had built his empire.

Chapter 15: The Town Decides

Blackwater Cove loved two things: money and scandal.

By the time Sarah returned home that afternoon, whispers had already begun. At the grocery store, at the marina, at the salon, everywhere.

The rich man's young wife.

The dead woman.

The neighbor.

And suspicion.

People didn't wait for answers. They filled in the gaps themselves.

A woman at the grocery store paused too long as Sarah passed, her cart half blocking the aisle. She didn't say anything, but her eyes lingered.

At the marina, two men speaking near the docks lowered their voices when Sarah walked by, their conversation cutting off mid-sentence.

Even at the edge of town, where the roads grew quieter and the wind carried less sound, she felt it.

The shift in atmosphere.

Not confrontation, but judgment forming quietly, like weather changing before a storm.

Sarah kept her eyes forward each time, pretending not to notice, but her pace quickened slightly as she walked.

Chapter 16: The Arrest

Three days later, the police returned.

This time, they didn't come with questions.

They came with handcuffs.

"Sarah Callahan, you are under arrest for the murder of Leslie Carter."

"No," Sarah whispered.

Her knees weakened.

Steven stood beside her, still.

Medina gently took Sarah's wrists. Cold metal clicked shut.

"Steven, I didn't do it," Sarah said desperately. "Please."

He didn't answer immediately.

"Don't answer questions," he finally said. "I'm calling a lawyer."

As Sarah was led out, she glanced back once at the house. The doorway framed Steven perfectly, unmoving, watching without expression.

A neighbor across the street had opened their curtain slightly, just enough to see.

The quiet of the neighborhood felt heavier than usual, as if even the air had slowed to observe.

The patrol car door closed with a final sound that echoed more than it should have.

Chapter 17: Laura Medina

Detective Laura Medina had seen guilty people before.

They avoided eye contact. They panicked. They lied poorly.

Sarah Callahan did none of those things.

She looked… shattered. She looked as sad and concerned as everyone in town.

That was what unsettled her.

That evening, Medina stood outside the station watching the sunset burn orange over the ocean.

Her partner joined her.

"Open and shut case," he said.

Medina didn't respond immediately.

"Have you met Steven Callahan?" she asked.

"Once. Powerful guy."

Medina narrowed her eyes slightly.

"Too powerful."

"What are you saying?"

Medina crossed her arms.

"I'm saying something about him bothers me."

Medina looked down at her notes again, flipping back through earlier pages. The pattern wasn't forming cleanly. Evidence existed, but it didn't feel anchored.

It felt placed.

Intentional.

Her partner misread her silence.

"You're overthinking it," he said lightly. "Billionaires bother everyone."

But Medina wasn't looking at the case anymore.

"No. It's something else."

She stared toward the horizon.

"I've seen innocent people before."

Her partner sighed. "You think Sarah is innocent?"

Medina spoke slowly.

She was looking at the structure around it. And structures, she knew, only held as long as the weakest point wasn't touched.

Somewhere in Blackwater Cove, someone had already chosen that weak point.

And she intended to find it.

In the massive mansion overlooking the ocean—

Steven Callahan sat alone in his office.

The police believed Sarah.

Soon the court would believe Sarah too.

Everything was unfolding exactly as he had planned.

But Steven had made one mistake.

He didn't know yet—

Detective Laura Medina had just started pulling at the thread.

And when the truth finally unraveled…

It would destroy everything.

Chapter 18: The Woman Everyone Hated

The jail cell was smaller than Sarah had imagined.

All it had was a cold metal bed, gray concrete walls, and a narrow window too high to see out of.

She sat on the edge of the bed, her arms wrapped around herself, trying to understand how her life had collapsed in less than a week, replaying every moment in her mind as if doing so might somehow change the outcome.

Leslie Carter was dead. And somehow, Sarah Callahan had become the murderer.

The silence inside the cell pressed down on her, heavy and suffocating, broken only by the occasional distant clang of metal doors and muffled voices from down the corridor. She had never felt so alone, so completely cut off from the life she once knew. Even the air felt different here, stale and unmoving, as though time itself had slowed down to a crawl.

Her thoughts drifted unwillingly back to Leslie, to the last time she had seen her alive, to the tension in her voice and the anger in her eyes. Sarah squeezed her eyes shut, trying to block it out, but memory refused to obey. Every detail returned sharper than before, making it impossible to escape the weight of it.

The guard opened the door.

"You have a visitor."

Sarah stood up slowly, exhausted by depression.

Her legs felt weak as she walked into the small visitor room, her heartbeat echoing loudly in her ears.

A tall man in a navy suit stood when she entered.

"Mrs. Callahan," he said politely. "I'm Daniel Wright."

Sarah frowned. "Thank God you are here," she said, her voice barely steady, as relief mixed with fear.

Daniel adjusted his tie.

"Mrs. Callahan, I am here because Mr. Callahan called me."

The words made her chest tighten.

Of course he did.

Steven liked to take care of everything right away, always appearing in control, always anticipating the next move before anyone else even realized there was one.

Daniel sat down across from her.

"I'm the best defense attorney in the state," he said calmly. "Your husband insisted you receive the strongest defense possible."

Sarah tried to speak, but her throat closed, her thoughts spiraling too fast to form words.

"Am I going to prison?" she whispered.

Daniel leaned forward, his expression measured and precise.

"That depends on how convincing we are," he said, choosing each word carefully, as if already building the case in his mind.

Sarah stared at him, searching his face for reassurance, but found only professionalism. For the first time, she realized that this was no longer about truth or innocence alone, it was about perception, strategy, and survival. And she had no idea how to survive any of it.

Daniel studied her for a moment longer, then slid a thin folder across the table. "We need to go over everything," he said. "Every conversation, every movement, every detail from that night."

Sarah hesitated before opening it, her hands trembling slightly. Seeing her life reduced to notes and bullet points felt surreal, like she was reading about someone else entirely. Yet every word carried consequences.

"I didn't do this," she said again, more firmly this time, as though saying it out aloud might make it more real.

Daniel nodded once, not in agreement, but in acknowledgment. "Then we make sure the court believes that," he replied.

But even as he spoke, Sarah could not shake the growing fear that the truth alone might not be enough.

Chapter 19: The Perfect Husband

The courtroom was packed.

Blackwater Cove had never seen a trial like this.

Reporters filled the back rows, and locals whispered from the benches, their curiosity sharpened into judgment as they watched every movement unfold. Some leaned forward eagerly, as if expecting a spectacle rather than a legal proceeding, while others exchanged knowing looks that suggested they had already made up their minds.

Across the room sat Nate. His face was tight with anger and grief, his eyes fixed on Sarah as though searching for answers she could not give.

Behind them sat Steven Callahan. His posture was perfect, his suit impeccable. He looked like the grieving husband, the supportive spouse, the man everyone respected, sitting with composed stillness that made him appear almost untouchable. Every movement he made was deliberate, controlled, reinforcing the image he had built over the years.

The case had everything the town loved.

Wealth, beauty, betrayal.

Whispers moved through the crowd like wind through dry leaves, carrying speculation and suspicion from one person to another.

Sarah kept her eyes forward, refusing to look at the faces that now stared at her with quiet condemnation.

She looked fragile, small.

Nothing like the monster the town had already decided she was.

The judge entered.

Everyone stood up.

"Be seated."

Sarah's lawyer, Daniel Wright, leaned slightly toward her.

"This is just the bond hearing," he whispered. "Stay calm."

Sarah nodded, though her stomach twisted painfully, her nerves tightening with every passing second.

"The prosecutor may begin," The judge nodded to the prosecutor.

"Ladies and gentlemen," the prosecutor began, "this case is about jealousy." He walked slowly across the courtroom, letting the weight of his words settle. "Sarah Callahan became close with Nate Reynolds."

Sarah shook her head softly, her denial almost invisible.

"But Nate had a girlfriend, Leslie Carter." The prosecutor turned toward the jury. "And when Leslie confronted Sarah…" He paused. "She died."

Gasps rippled through the room.

Steven lowered his head slightly, the image of grief perfectly displayed.

Nate was looking at her in disbelief, his expression shifting between confusion and suspicion.

Across the aisle, Detective Medina watched him closely, her sharp gaze missing nothing.

Then the prosecutor added. "Your Honor, the state requests that the defendant be held without bail."

A murmur spread through the courtroom.

Sarah's head snapped up. *Without bail?*

Daniel Wright stood immediately. "Your Honor, my client has no criminal record. She is a long-time resident of this community and poses no flight risk. She has agreed to submit her travel documents to the court if required. There's no need for physical remand of my client."

The prosecutor walked slowly toward the judge's bench.

"This is a murder investigation," he said firmly. "The evidence places Mrs. Callahan at the crime scene, and the state believes releasing her could compromise the ongoing investigation."

Sarah felt the room closing in around her, her breath becoming shallow.

Daniel spoke again. "My client deserves the opportunity to defend herself while free."

The judge leaned forward, hands folded. He studied Sarah carefully, his expression unreadable. Then he spoke. "Given the severity of the charges and the evidence presented, and her resources that could make her a flight risk, the court denies bail at this time." The words hit Sarah like a physical blow. "Mrs. Callahan will remain in custody until trial."

Gasps spread through the courtroom.

Sarah turned toward Steven instinctively. He sat in the gallery, perfectly composed. Their eyes met for a brief moment. Something about his expression made her chest tighten. There was no panic. No desperation. He had a calculated expression.

The bailiff stepped forward.

"Mrs. Callahan, please stand."

Cold metal cuffs closed around her wrists again, the sound sharp and final.

As she was led away, Sarah finally understood the reality of what was happening, and how quickly everything she trusted had unraveled. She wasn't going home. Not tonight. Maybe not for a very long time.

As she passed the rows of spectators, she could feel their eyes on her, hear the faint whispers that followed in her wake. To them, she was no longer a neighbor or a friend, she was a headline, a story to be told and retold.

Somewhere in the courtroom behind her, Steven Callahan watched silently, his stillness more unsettling than any visible emotion.

Just as he had planned.

Chapter 20: Nate's Doubt

Nate couldn't sleep. Leslie's voice haunted him, echoing in fragments of memory that refused to settle into silence.

He wished the last thing that had happened between them wasn't that petty fight, a meaningless argument that now felt unbearably insignificant. If he had known it would be their last conversation, he would have said something different, something better.

He sat at his desk, staring at his laptop, his mind racing as he tried to make sense of everything.

News articles. Timelines. Speculation.

Each one seemed to twist the truth into something unrecognizable, turning real events into something distorted and incomplete.

He opened the security footage of the night Leslie had died from the camera outside his house. He had already provided this footage to Detective Medina. It was part of her investigation, he had to. But today he wanted to see it himself.

The footage showed Leslie leaving the house around 10:42 p.m.. She walked toward the cliff road, her figure small against the darkness. Ten minutes later, a car drove slowly down the street. Nate leaned closer to the screen, his pulse quickening as unease crept in. The car was black. A luxury sedan. He recognized it instantly. It was Steven Callahan's car. Nate's stomach dropped, a cold realization forming in the pit of his gut.

Something didn't make sense. Why did Steven follow her in the direction of the cliffs? Was he watching her? Could it he have murdered her? But why?

Nate ran his hands through his hair, frustration building as questions piled on top of one another without answers. Steven had always seemed composed, controlled, almost too perfect. Now that perfection felt suspicious, like a carefully constructed mask hiding something darker underneath.

He replayed the footage again, watching every second more carefully, searching for anything he might have missed the first time. The slow, deliberate movement of the car, the timing, the direction, none of it felt like coincidence anymore.

He paused the video and zoomed in, trying to catch a clearer look at the license plate, but the angle and lighting made it difficult. Still, he did not need confirmation, he knew that car. A new thought crept in, one that made his chest tighten. If Steven was there, then Sarah might not be the one responsible.

The idea shifted everything.

For the first time, Nate felt the weight of doubt pressing in from a different direction, forcing him to question not just the events of that night, but the narrative that had already begun to take shape around them. And once that doubt took hold, it refused to let go.

Chapter 21: The First Crack

Detective Medina sat alone in her office, reviewing Steven's statement. The timeline seemed perfect, almost too perfect, laid out in a way that anticipated scrutiny and attempted to eliminate it entirely.

Steven claimed he had been home the entire night Leslie died, watching television with Sarah, presenting himself as calm and cooperative.

But something in Medina's mind wouldn't settle. She had seen too many cases, too many carefully constructed alibis that unraveled under scrutiny, to accept perfection at face value. She opened the Callahan security file.

Steven had provided footage from his home cameras to prove he had never left. But Medina noticed something strange. A time gap. Between 10:30 and 11:55 PM. The footage skipped, cutting out nearly an hour and a half of time. It was enough to miss something important.

Medina leaned back slowly, her instincts sharpening as the inconsistency took hold.

"That's interesting," she murmured.

Wealthy men like Steven didn't usually make mistakes, especially not ones that could be discovered so easily. Unless they believed no one would look closely enough.

She leaned forward again, studying the timestamps, replaying the footage, and noting the exact moment the gap had begun and ended. It was too clean to be accidental, too convenient to ignore.

Medina reached for her notebook and began writing down questions, each one building toward a clearer picture.

Where was Steven during that missing time?

Why remove that portion of the footage?

And perhaps most importantly, what had he done that he didn't want anyone to see?

She stood up and walked over to the window of her office, staring out at the quiet town beyond. Blackwater Cove looked peaceful on the surface, but she knew better. Beneath that calm exterior, something was shifting.

Returning to her desk, she picked up the phone, considering her next move. This kind of detail could not be ignored, and it certainly could not be left unverified.

For the first time since the case had begun, Medina felt a shift. A small crack in the surface of a story that had seemed airtight before. She knew from experience that once a crack appeared, it rarely stayed small for long.

Chapter 22: The Story Begins to Collapse

The next day in court, Daniel Wright stood to cross-examine the lead investigator. The courtroom felt heavier than before, as if everyone could sense that something in the case was beginning to shift.

"Detective," he said smoothly, "is it true that there were no witnesses placing my client at the crime scene?"

The detective hesitated, glancing briefly at the prosecutor before answering.

"Yes."

"And was there any physical evidence besides the necklace and the wallet?"

"No."

Daniel turned toward the jury, allowing a deliberate pause to settle over the room.

"The entire case against Sarah Callahan depends on a necklace and her wallet that could have been placed there by anyone."

The prosecutor quickly objected.

"Sustained," the judge said.

But the seed had already been planted. The jurors exchanged subtle looks, and one of them shifted uncomfortably in their seat.

Daniel returned to his table, his expression calm, but his strategy was clear. He was not trying to prove Sarah's innocence outright. He was simply creating enough uncertainty to fracture the prosecution's narrative.

Across the room, Steven watched quietly. His expression never changed, but his mind moved quickly.

Daniel Wright was doing exactly what Steven expected, creating doubt and making the case messy. Because the messier it became, the easier it would be to control the outcome.

Steven leaned back slightly, his fingers resting lightly on the table as if everything were proceeding according to plan. He had anticipated resistance, but not collapse.

What Steven did not know was that Detective Medina was already following a different thread, one that led straight back to him. As she observed the exchange, her instincts sharpened. The cracks in the case were not random. They were deliberate, and she intended to find out who had created them.

Chapter 23: The Detective's Instinct

Medina sat across from Nate Reynolds in a quiet diner near the marina. The hum of conversation around them created a sense of privacy, even in the open space.

"Why did you ask to meet me?" she asked.

Nate slid his laptop across the table.

"I found something."

Medina leaned forward as he opened the file. He played the security footage.

The black sedan rolled slowly down the street, its movement almost deliberate.

Medina's eyes narrowed.

"Do you know whose car that is?" Nate asked.

Medina did not answer immediately, because she already knew.

Steven Callahan.

She studied the footage again, paying attention to the timing, the angle, and the way the car lingered just long enough to suggest intent.

"Do you suspect that Leslie had an affair with Steven?" she asked.

"No, I don't think so," Nate replied firmly.

"Then why do you think he followed her?"

"I don't know. I am asking myself the same questions. She never mentioned any threats or anything about Steven."

Medina sat back, her mind already connecting pieces that did not seem obvious at first glance. This was not about an affair. It felt more controlled, more calculated.

Patterns mattered, and this felt like one.

Medina excused herself, standing up slowly. "If there is anything else, please don't hesitate to contact me," she said.

As she walked out of the diner, her thoughts sharpened. The car in the footage was not just passing by. It was watching. Waiting.

And that meant Steven was not just involved. He was paying attention in ways that did not fit the story being presented in court.

Chapter 24: Steven Feels the Shift

Steven noticed the change before anyone said it. He always did. Detective Medina looked at him differently in court that day, longer, sharper, almost like she wanted to confront him about some suspicion.

Steven recognized this look instantly. He had seen many times in business negotiations. It was when a person was beginning to question the story.

Steven remained calm, maintaining the same composed posture he had perfected over the years. But inside, something tightened.

He had controlled every variable, every witness, and every piece of evidence.

So why did he suddenly feel like the ground was shifting beneath him?

He adjusted his cufflinks, a small, practiced gesture that helped him maintain focus. Control was not just something he had exercised over others. It was something he had imposed on himself.

Across the courtroom, Detective Medina met his gaze. There was no hesitation in her eyes now, only quiet certainty. And for the first time since Leslie Carter had died, Steven Callahan felt something unfamiliar.

Fear. Fear of losing.

It unsettled him more than anything else. Not because he had never faced challenges, but because this felt different. This felt personal.

He told himself it was temporary, just another complication to manage. But deep down, he knew something had shifted.

And once control began to slip, it rarely returned the same way again.

Chapter 25: Steven's Secret

Detective Medina spent the next two days digging into Steven Callahan's past. Powerful men always had secrets. The trick was finding the one they feared most.

Steven's public life was spotless, filled with successful business deals, charity donations, and political connections. But Medina knew where to look. She dug up his private records, old lawsuits, and digital traces.

She worked late into the night, combing through archived data and piecing together fragments that most people would overlook. And then she found something. There was a pattern in Steven's internet history recovered from a deleted server backup.

There were late-night searches, hundreds of them, not about Sarah, and not about Leslie. They were all about Nate. About his company, his net worth, his social media, and his photos. He had opened up and looked at all his pictures, even older ones from years before Nate had moved to Blackwater Cove.

Medina leaned back in her chair slowly. Steven had not been watching Sarah. He had been watching Nate. This realization changed everything. This was not about jealousy in the traditional sense. It was something deeper, something more obsessive.

She began to map the timeline, comparing searches with real-world events. The consistency was undeniable. Steven had been tracking Nate for years, long before any of this began. Medina's instincts sharpened further.

Could it be that he felt threatened by Nate, or was it something far more complicated?

Either way, she knew she was getting closer to the truth.

Chapter 26: Leslie's Discovery

Leslie Carter had figured it out the night she had died. It was a detail the investigation finally uncovered through a voice memo on her phone, a recording she had made earlier that evening. Her voice trembled slightly as she spoke.

"I think Steven is obsessed with Nate. He is not jealous, it's something else." The recording crackled. "I saw him watching Nate through binoculars. Not Sarah. He was watching Nate… Watching every single move Nate made…"

There was silence for a moment, followed by the faint sound of movement in the background.

Then Leslie whispered, "This was never about Sarah."

The recording ended.

Medina stared at the screen, letting the weight of the words settle in.

Everything suddenly made sense. The jealousy, the framing, the murder. Steven had not killed Leslie out of anger. He killed her because she had seen the truth.

Medina replayed the recording again, focusing on the tone in Leslie's voice. It was not just fear. It was realization.

Leslie had understood something that no one else had, and it had cost her life. The clarity of the motive shifted the entire case. This was no longer circumstantial. This was personal. And now, Medina knew exactly what she was dealing with.

Chapter 27: The Trap

Medina met Nate and Sarah separately.

Sarah looked exhausted but determined, her eyes reflecting both fear and resolve. "You're suspecting that Steven killed her?" Sarah asked quietly.

Medina nodded.

"And blamed me for it?"

"Yes."

Nate clenched his jaw.

"What do we do?"

Medina's eyes hardened.

"We make him confess."

They designed a trap. They planned a conversation staged between Nate and Sarah in a public place where Steven's cameras could hear everything. They would make Steven believe the truth was about to come out.

Medina carefully explained every detail, from where they would stand to how loudly they needed to speak. Timing was critical.

"And what if he doesn't show?" Sarah asked.

"He will," Medina replied confidently.

"Why?" Nate asked.

"Because people like Steven cannot tolerate losing control."

The plan required precision, but more importantly, it required trust.

Sarah hesitated for a moment, then nodded.

She had already lost too much to back down now. If Steven was truly behind Leslie's murder, he was not going to save her because it was either him or Sarah and he would always save himself. And she also knew that men like Steven only had one reaction when their control slipped.

They panicked. Detective Medina was tight, he will show up.

Chapter 28: The Breaking Point

That night, Sarah met Nate at the marina pier.

Steven watched through the camera feed in his office. His heart began beating faster. Something was wrong.

Nate leaned toward Sarah. "Leslie knew," Nate said loudly.

Steven froze.

"She figured out Steven was obsessed with you," Sarah replied.

Steven's hands trembled.

"You think he killed her?" Nate asked.

"Yes," Sarah said.

"And if the police hear that recording Leslie made…"

Steven stood up suddenly. The chair behind him crashed to the floor. His entire life had been built on control. And control was slipping.

Across the street, Nate and Sarah continued the conversation exactly as Medina had instructed, carefully following the script while making it sound natural.

Steven could not hear the police vehicles quietly approaching. All he could hear was his own fear. It filled his chest, drowning out reason. He grabbed his car keys.

If Sarah told the police, everything would be destroyed.

He rushed out, barely remembering to lock the door behind him. For the first time in years, Steven was not thinking strategically. He was reacting. And that made him dangerous.

Chapter 29: The Truth

Steven drove to the marina like a man chasing his own shadow. When he stepped onto the pier, Nate and Sarah turned. Steven's face was pale, his composure cracking under pressure.

"You shouldn't be talking about things you don't understand," he said quietly.

Sarah's voice trembled. "You killed Leslie."

Steven laughed bitterly. "She was going to ruin everything."

Nate stepped forward. "Everything, or your reputation?"

Steven's eyes snapped toward him. "You think you understand?" Steven said. His voice cracked for the first time. "My entire life is built on being well respected. If she had told anyone, I'd be ruined!"

Police lights flashed behind him, casting long shadows across the pier.

Steven did not notice.

"I couldn't be what I am," he continued. "Not in this town. Not with my name."

Sarah's eyes widened.

"You killed her because she knew you were gay?"

Steven looked at Nate, the truth finally spilling out. "She saw me watching him," Steven whispered.

Nate felt his stomach drop.

Steven's voice trembled. "She was going to tell people. She would have destroyed everything."

The weight of his confession hung in the air.

For a moment, everything felt still. Then Medina stepped forward from the darkness.

"Steven Callahan," she said calmly, "you're under arrest."

Steven turned slowly. For the first time in decades, he had lost control. And there was no way to get it back.

Chapter 30: The Fall of a Powerful Man

The courtroom was silent as the verdict was read. The atmosphere felt heavy, as if the entire room was holding its breath, waiting for the moment that would change everything.

Steven Callahan sat rigid in his chair, his hands clenched tightly together. His reputation had collapsed overnight, leaving behind a man who no longer resembled the image he had carefully built over decades. The town that once worshipped him now stared at him like a stranger, as if they were struggling to reconcile the man they admired with the man standing trial.

"Guilty of murder."

Gasps filled the room, echoing off the wooden walls and high ceiling of the courtroom.

Steven didn't react. He simply stared ahead, his expression frozen, as officers stepped forward and placed handcuffs on his wrists. The metallic sound seemed louder than it should have been, marking the end of an era.

Across the courtroom, Sarah shut her eyes in relief, finally allowing herself to breathe after days of tension and fear. Nate exhaled slowly, his expression unreadable but calm. Detective Medina stood still, watching the man who once believed he controlled everything finally lose his grip on power, influence, and identity.

As Steven was led away, the judge's final words echoed through the room with finality.

"The court hereby sentences you to life imprisonment without the possibility of parole, to be served for the remainder of your natural life."

Steven Callahan had spent decades protecting his image, building it carefully like a fortress. In the end, that same image had become the weapon that destroyed him. What he never considered was how fragile control becomes when truth begins to surface, piece by piece, until there is nothing left to hold it together.

Outside the courtroom, life continued, but for those inside, everything had changed forever.

Chapter 31: Hidden Truth

Steven believed he had killed Leslie to protect his reputation. That belief had become the foundation of his defense in his own mind, a justification he repeated silently to preserve what little sense of control he had left. That part was true, at least from his perspective.

But what he never realized was that someone had quietly pushed events in that direction. Someone had understood Steven's psychology perfectly, knowing exactly how he would react under pressure, fear, and perceived betrayal. Someone had not forced his hand directly, but had shaped the circumstances around him with precision.

Someone who knew how to provoke him.

Nate Reynolds.

Steven never saw the manipulation because it never appeared as force. It appeared as coincidence, timing, and emotional escalation. Every interaction, every subtle pressure point had been carefully placed until Steven's own instincts completed the final step.

Nate did not need to act openly. He only needed Steven to believe he was acting alone. And that was the most dangerous kind of control.

In the aftermath, Detective Medina would later review the case files and begin noticing inconsistencies that no one had questioned at the time. Patterns of behavior, emotional triggers, and strategic positioning all pointed toward something deeper than a simple crime of passion. It suggested planning, patience, and psychological understanding.

Steven had fallen, but not in the way the town believed. His downfall was not only the result of guilt, but also orchestration. And the truth, buried beneath legal proceedings and public judgment, was far more complex than anyone wanted to admit.

Epilogue: The Man Across the Street

Six months later.

The mansion across the street stood empty now. The Callahan estate had been sold quietly after Steven's conviction, its presence erased from the town's daily conversation as if it had never mattered at all.

Sarah stood near the marina, watching the sunset over Blackwater Cove. The ocean glowed deep orange as waves rolled slowly toward the cliffs, their motion steady and indifferent to human consequence. The wind carried the scent of salt and distance, as if urging her toward something new.

Behind her, Nate approached quietly.

"You really leaving tomorrow?" he asked.

Sarah nodded. "I can't stay here anymore."

Nate understood without needing an explanation. This town had nearly destroyed her sense of safety, trust, and identity. Even though justice had been served, the emotional weight remained.

"You deserved better," he said softly.

Sarah smiled faintly.

"Maybe."

They stood in silence for a moment, watching the horizon fade into evening light. The world felt larger now, but also emptier.

Then Sarah looked at him. "Thank you for believing me when no one else did."

Nate gave a gentle nod. "Of course."

But inside his mind, something colder stirred, something that had nothing to do with relief or closure.

Because the truth was, Nate had believed Sarah was innocent long before anyone else did. Not because he trusted her in the way most people understand trust, but because he had known the outcome long before it arrived.

He had been watching Steven from the moment he moved into town. Studying him carefully, understanding patterns, reactions, weaknesses. And most importantly, shaping the path that would lead Steven exactly where he needed him to go.

Nate Reynolds had not moved to Blackwater Cove by accident.

Years earlier, Steven Callahan's business empire had destroyed Nate's father financially. The collapse had not been sudden, but slow and humiliating, stripping away stability, dignity, and hope. The scandal that followed ruined his father's life in ways no public record fully captured.

Six months later, his father took his own life. Nate never forgot the name responsible.

Steven Callahan.

That name became a fixed point in his life, something he could never ignore or forgive. Over time, grief turned into calculation. Pain turned into focus. Focus turned into planning.

So Nate did what Steven had always done to others. He built a plan. A slow one. A careful one.

When Nate bought the house across the street, it was not for the ocean view or the quiet neighborhood. It was proximity, access, and opportunity. It was about understanding Steven from within his own environment, observing him in his natural state, and waiting for the moment when pressure would break him.

Everything that followed was not random. It was design.

Sarah turned to Nate again as the evening wind picked up. "I hope Steven rots in prison," she said quietly.

Nate looked out at the ocean. The waves crashed endlessly against the cliffs where Leslie died, carrying with them the memory of what had happened but never fully revealing it.

Steven Callahan's life was over. His empire destroyed. His reputation erased. Everything he had built over decades had collapsed in a matter of weeks.

Justice had been served. But not by the law, and not by chance. It had been served by patience, and by revenge carefully disguised as coincidence.

Sarah hugged Nate goodbye before leaving, holding onto the moment as if it might anchor her to something stable before she moved on. She never noticed the slight smile on his face. And she never asked the question that would have terrified her most.

Why Nate Reynolds had really moved into the house across the street?

9 781972 458259